Introducing

BACH

ROLAND VERNON

First published in the UK in 1995 by
Belitha Press Limited
31 Newington Green, London N16 9PU

Copyright © 1996 this edition by Silver Burdett Press
    A Division of Simon & Schuster
  299 Jefferson Road
  Parsippany, New Jersey 07054

Printed in Singapore for Imago

1 2 3 4 5 6 7 8 9 10

Editor: Claire Edwards
Designer: Andrew Oliver
Picture researcher: Juliet Duff

Library of Congress Cataloging-in-Publication Data
Vernon, Roland, 1961-
    Introducing Bach/Roland Vernon.
        p.   cm.
    Originally published: London:Belitha Press. 1995
    Includes index.
    Summary: Examines the childhood and early musical training of the prolific eighteenth-century German composer as well as the influences and historical events that shaped his adult life.

ISBN 0-382-39157-8 (LSB)   –   ISBN 0-382-39155-1 (pbk.)

    1. Bach, Johann Sebastian, 1685-1750—Juvenile literature. 2. Composers—Germany—Biography—Juvenile literature. [1. Bach, Johann Sebastian,—1685-1750. 2. Composers.] I. Title.
ML3930.B2V47 1995 95-10911
780'.92—dc20CIP
    AC MN

Picture Acknowledgments:
AKG, London: Front Cover, Back cover right, title page, 6 top, 8 top left, 10 bottom right, 12 both, 13 top, 17 top, 20–21, 21 right, 22 top, 25 both, 26 top, 28 bottom
Bildarchiv Preussischer Kulturbesitz: 8 top right, 18 bottom.
Bridgeman Art Library: 6 left Kunsthistorisches Museum, Vienna, 7 right City of Bristol Museum and Art Gallery, 11 bottom Louvre, Paris/Giraudon, 13 bottom Christie's, London, 14 top Santa Maria della Vittoria, Rome, 16 top Schloss Museum, Weimar, 18 top Private Collection, 26–7 bottom Staatliche Museen zu Berlin, 17 top Burg Hohenstollern, Hechingen.
ET Archive: 14 bottom, 28 top.
Mary Evans Picture Library: Back page left.
Germanisches Nationalmuseum, Nürnberg: 24.
Reproduced by Courtesy of the Trustees of the National Gallery, London: 19 top.
Pictorial Press: 29 top.
Science Photo Library: 29 bottom NASA.
Stadtgeschichtsmuseum, Arnstadt/Foto Sallatsch: 11 top.
Zefa: 8 bottom, 15 bottom

CONTENTS

Fig. 83. — CARILLON WITH CLAVIER.
Width, 15.44 in.

INTRODUCING BACH

JOHANN SEBASTIAN BACH is nowadays seen as the wise old man of music, perhaps even the greatest composer of all. But Bach would have been surprised at this. He wrote music for the glory of God, and to satisfy his own burning curiosity, not for future fame. In fact, during his life most people knew him as a brilliant organist, not as a composer. He never traveled outside Germany and was content just to carry out his duties as a working musician. Tradition was very special to Bach: the musical tradition of his family, the religious tradition of his country, and traditional ways of composing. These were more important to him than the changing fashions of music. Bach did not set out to change the world, but he brought the music of the past to new and glorious heights. His work is vast and complex. There is no other composer to compare with him.

Music
in the family

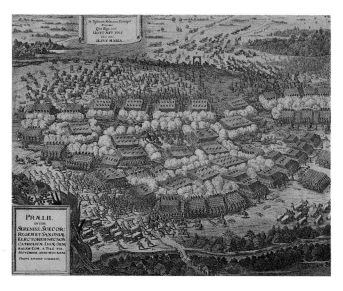

The Battle of Breitenfeld in 1631, fought near Leipzig, was part of the Thirty Years' War.

Before Bach's birth, Europe had been torn apart in a struggle for power, and the German **Reich** was devastated. For 30 years the Emperor Ferdinand II had fought a bitter war against his enemies—Denmark and Sweden in the north, France and the Netherlands in the west. There was also a rebellion within Germany itself, led by **Protestant** noblemen who felt threatened by their Emperor's strong Catholic beliefs.

The year 1648 brought an end to the **Thirty Years' War**, but the Holy Roman Emperor had lost much of his power over the 300 or more small states that made up the empire. From then on this huge jigsaw of cities and territories was actually governed by local rulers—church leaders, town councils, or noblemen.

Ferdinand II (1578–1637), the Holy Roman Emperor.

Musicians at this time were the servants of these rulers. Their job was to provide music for religious events, city festivities, or court entertainment.

In the central German state of Thuringia, one particular family produced several generations of skilled musicians. This was the Bach family. As music began to be played again after the years of war, the Bach family's fame started to grow. Soon in Thuringia the name "Bach" began to mean the same as "musician." Once a year the whole family would gather for a huge meeting. Brothers, uncles, great uncles, and distant cousins would be there. They would play music together and discuss family business. It was like a private musicians' **guild**, and most children born into the family were expected to join.

Martin Luther (1483–1546), the great religious reformer, had also lived in Thuringia. The many hymns he wrote helped to build up a tradition of church music in that part of Germany. He believed that music could help teach people about God. The Bach family also saw music as a way of expressing their faith.

A meeting of the Bach family. Many of Sebastian's relations were professional musicians.

Martin Luther

A THIRST FOR KNOWLEDGE

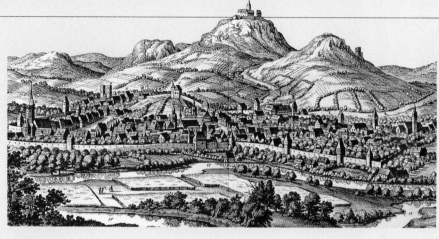

Above: Johann Ambrosius Bach, Sebastian's father.

Above right: Eisenach, as Bach's parents would have known it.

Below: The Wartburg Castle and Eisenach as they are today.

On March 21, 1685, Johann Ambrosius Bach and his wife, Elisabeth, had their eighth child. They probably expected that the young Johann Sebastian would be a good musician, like almost everyone else in the family. They may not have guessed that hundreds of years later he would be seen as one of the greatest composers ever.

Bach was born in the town of Eisenach, near Wartburg Castle, where Luther had been held for his safety in 1521. His father was a successful musician, who performed **ceremonial** music at the town hall and later took on a second job, as court musician for the local duke. He made sure that he gave his children a solid musical education, specializing in the violin, which he played himself. Another relative, Johann Christoph Bach, was in charge of the town's church music. Sebastian would sit next to him in the organ loft, inspired by his playing and the music he wrote. Before long, Sebastian became an experienced **chorister**.

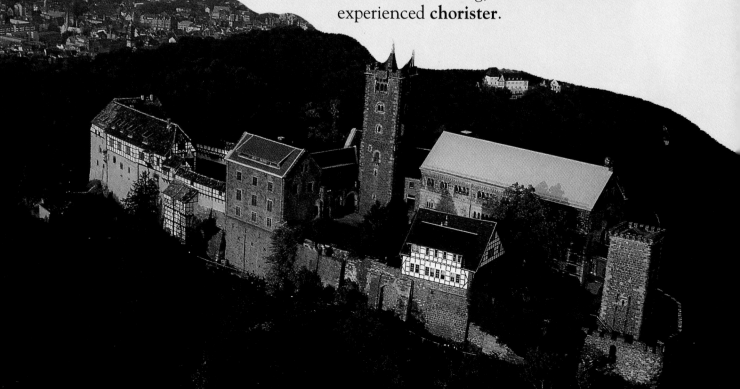

At the age of eight, the young Bach went to the Latin School, where Luther had been taught, but his life in Eisenach was suddenly struck by tragedy. His parents died within nine months of each other, in 1694 and 1695. Orphaned and homeless, he went to live with his eldest brother Christoph, who was organist in the town of Ohrdruf. Christoph gave him lessons on the organ and taught him the basic rules of musical composition.

Sebastian was thirsty for knowledge. He was a brilliant pupil both at school and at home. There is a story that his brother had a book of pieces by famous composers, and that Sebastian was not allowed to study it because it was thought to be too difficult for a 12-year-old. He managed to get hold of the book anyway, and secretly copied out its contents by moonlight. His brother eventually found out and confiscated both the book and Sebastian's copy.

A YOUNG MAN WITH NEW IDEAS

Christoph by now had his own children and could no longer afford to give his brother a home. So in 1700 Sebastian left Ohrdruf to finish his education in the town of Lüneburg, 150 miles away. He won a **choral scholarship** to the choir school of St. Michael's Church, which gave him somewhere to live and paid his school fees.

He sang in the choir until his voice broke, and then played the violin in the orchestra. The standard of performance was very high, and he could not have hoped for better training. He also spent hours in the school library, studying past composers and traditional methods of composing, including **polyphony**. Meanwhile, his organ playing improved with lessons from the famous organist Georg Böhm.

In 1703, at the age of 18, Sebastian returned to Thuringia to look for a job. The Bach family had worked for years in Arnstadt, and Sebastian became organist at the New Church there. He was well paid, and the church had a good new organ.

A bassoon player in the early eighteenth century.

Bach's organ at the New Church, Arnstadt. Bach was at first asked just to look at ways to improve the organ. He carried out his task so well, he was invited to stay on as organist.

An organist in those days was supposed to write his own music for church services, but some of Bach's music startled people. He would often **improvise** brilliant new versions of traditional hymn tunes, making them up as he went along. People complained that his playing was too fancy and that the hymns were too difficult to follow.

This annoyed Bach, and so did the bad behavior of his choristers, many of whom were older than he was and impossible to control. He even had a fight with a bassoon player, whom he accused of sounding like a nanny goat.

The situation became worse when he took four months off to visit the great organist composer **Buxtehude** in the distant town of Lübeck. He walked back the 199 miles to Arnstadt to face a furious town council. They said he'd been away too long, his playing was more complicated than ever, and, worse still, he had been heard talking with a female singer in the organ loft. This was against the rules, and Bach was asked to explain himself.

LOUIS XIV AND THE WAR OF THE SPANISH SUCCESSION

Bach would have been used to the sight of soldiers coming and going, as there were many wars in Europe throughout his life. One of the most important was fought against King Louis XIV of France. Louis (1638–1715) was both a brutal and a brilliant ruler, whose reign was marked by war. He was more interested in the power and influence of France than the happiness of his people. During his reign France became the leader of Europe, and he was known as the Sun King.

In 1701 Louis went to war with the Holy Roman Emperor and England, over who should inherit the crown of Spain. For many years Spain had been ruled by relatives of the Emperor, but Louis wanted it for his grandson. After 13 years of war, peace was signed. The French royal family kept Spain but lost much of their power and land. Louis died soon after, a broken old man. Many people in France felt that their king had let them down.

AN ORGAN VIRTUOSO

The young woman in the organ loft was probably Maria Barbara Bach, one of Sebastian's second cousins, and, like the rest of her family, a good musician. A year later she married Sebastian, but by this time he had left his job at Arnstadt. He was tired of working with a second-rate choir, and he felt that the council did not appreciate his music. So he looked around Thuringia for a new job, and in 1707 became organist at the Church of St. Blaise, Mühlhausen. Here he hoped for greater freedom to explore his ideas and to compose more challenging music.

By now Bach was well-known locally as an organ **virtuoso**. He understood all about how an organ worked and was often asked to give advice on ways the instrument's sound could be improved. He wrote two different kinds of organ music at this time. One was based on traditional **chorales**, or hymns, to which Bach added **variations** and **preludes**. The well-known tune stayed the same, but he added new tunes over the top. This is known as **counterpoint**. A later example of this is his famous version of the Advent chorale, "Wachet Auf" or "Sleepers Wake."

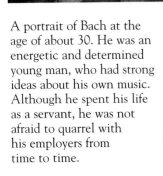

A portrait of Bach at the age of about 30. He was an energetic and determined young man, who had strong ideas about his own music. Although he spent his life as a servant, he was not afraid to quarrel with his employers from time to time.

An organist in the early eighteenth century. Bach was an outstanding organist, who was famous for being able to play complicated music at great speed without mistakes. His little finger was as strong and could move as quickly as his index finger.

Buxtehude is shown in this painting leaning against his hand, with J.A. Reinken (another great organist, whom Bach admired) playing the keyboard. Bach wanted to succeed Buxtehude as organist at Lübeck, but there was a condition: he would have to marry the man's daughter. Bach could not agree to this.

Bach's other type of organ music was more free in style, with grand effects and dramatic contrasts. Bach had learned much of this from the music of Buxtehude. One of the boldest of these pieces is his **Toccata** and **Fugue** in D minor, which uses the organ's many different types of sounds to the full.

But Bach left Mühlhausen within a year. The pay was small, and the pastor of the Church of St. Blaise was a **Pietist**, who preferred church music to be very simple. Bach resigned, saying that he wanted to write music that would "exalt the glory of God." He felt that Mühlhausen no longer offered him that opportunity.

THE CANTATA

A cantata literally means a piece of music to be sung. But Bach's cantatas usually had several different sections written for a combination of instruments, chorus, and solo singers. He wrote hundreds of cantatas, mostly for the church, but many for **secular** celebrations as well. Some are lost, but enough survive to show how Bach developed the cantata as no other composer has done.

Cantatas were traditionally used in the Lutheran Church as a way of teaching people the Bible. Bach later set religious poetry to music as well as quotations from the Bible. Each piece of music was carefully composed to match the words. Every chorus, **aria**, or **recitative** had a different mood, so that the finished product was more like **opera** than church music. An early example, *God Is My King*, was composed in Mühlhausen. The cantata was too splendid for the pastor of the Church of St. Blaise. He felt that such stirring music might stop people from thinking about God.

This manuscript of a cantata shows us Bach's musical handwriting.

ℬACH
AND THE BAROQUE

Around 1630 a new artistic movement, known as the Baroque, began in Rome and eventually spread to the whole of Europe. The Baroque joined together the arts of painting, architecture, and sculpture to create new and powerful effects. Artists designed the insides and outsides of churches to lift people's spirits and take their breath away. Yet everything was carefully organized to fit into a perfect pattern. To ordinary people, these buildings must have seemed as glorious as heaven, which is exactly what the artists wanted them to think.

Works such as **Bernini**'s *St. Theresa* are typical of the Italian Baroque. The huge sculpture seems to float upward on a cloud, and the light comes from above in dramatic shafts of gold. These, together with the saint's expression, bring the scene to life like a dazzling piece of theater.

The picture above shows Bernini's *The Ecstasy of St. Theresa* (1644–1647), a Baroque master-

GEORGE FRIDERIC HANDEL (1685–1759)

Handel was another great composer of the Baroque, but although he was born less than a month before Bach, and only 81 miles away, the two men never met. Their careers took them in different directions. Handel's fame spread to many countries, while Bach remained a local craftsman.

Like Bach, Handel started out as a virtuoso organist, but after a four-year visit to Italy, he became known as a composer of opera. He made many powerful friends. One of these was the Elector of Hanover, who later became King George I of England. The Elector employed him as music director at his court. But Handel saw better opportunities in England, and often went on leave to try out his operas in London. When the Elector came to England as king, Handel became a British subject and was made a royal composer. After many years of success, he turned to composing popular **oratorios**. The best-known of these is the *Messiah*, which is about the life of Jesus. Handel was buried in Westminster Abbey, London.

Although the Baroque was originally Italian, it became popular in other Roman Catholic countries. Louis XIV used it in his grand palaces, such as Versailles, in France. But Louis's idea was to glorify himself, rather than God!

After France, the rest of northern Europe took up the Baroque, and its influence spread to music as well. Bach and Handel are the two most famous composers of Baroque music. The drama in their music, the contrasts between soft and strong, chorus and solo, voices and instruments, are all typical of the Baroque style.

A work such as Bach's **Magnificat** sweeps us away with its splendor, just like some of the buildings of the time. The great Austrian monastery at Melk, for example, is set high on a rock above the Danube River and looks like a fairy-tale castle. Inside the church, statues, arches, domes, paintings, altars, and ornaments come together in a swirl of gold and light.

No wonder the German princes wanted the same style for their own palaces. They employed architects to design extravagant buildings that took the Baroque further than it had ever gone in Italy.

The monastery of Melk, in Austria, was begun in 1702. Baroque architects were beginning to understand that buildings could look even more magnificent if they were built in the right landscape. Melk, which is a Catholic monastery, looks particularly impressive, perched on the top of its massive rock. The position was carefully chosen because, at this time, Catholics were feeling threatened by the strength of Lutheranism.

THE COURT AT WEIMAR

(above) Wilhelm Ernst, Duke of
Saxe-Weimar (1662–1728).

In July 1708, Bach was appointed court organist and chamber musician to Duke Wilhelm Ernst of Saxe-Weimar. This was very different from being employed by town authorities, and Bach was given a uniform to wear, like a household servant. The duke was a very strict and religious man, but liked to encourage good music in his small **duchy**. Bach had to provide music for the palace chapel and play in the court orchestra at concerts.

He now had more freedom to compose, and most of his great organ works were written during his years at Weimar. Bach was also expected to write cantatas for the chapel, and his beautiful chorale arrangement known as "Jesu, Joy of Man's Desiring" comes from one of them. Another famous **melody**, "Sheep May Safely Graze," was also written at this time, but not for the church. It was part of a secular work, known as the *Hunt Cantata*, which was written for a duke's birthday.

Bach, teaching one of his sons, continues the tradition of music in the family.

By now Bach's outstanding skills as an organist had made him a celebrity. A grand public competition was arranged to test his skills against those of a famous visiting French organist, Louis Marchand. In the event, Marchand did not turn up. He left town mysteriously by the early morning coach, presumably because he was nervous of his rival. All this fame brought Bach many pupils, and he began to write a collection of simple compositions for them, which he called the *Little Organ Book*. This was the start of a lifelong dedication to teaching.

A concert at an eighteenth-century prince's court. The prince, dressed in red, has joined the musicians and can be seen playing a **viola da gamba**. A court was usually a cultural center for the arts, and a place where musicians could find employment.

When Duke Wilhelm Ernst's **Kapellmeister** died, Bach expected to be given the job. But the senior post went to the old man's son, so Bach resigned. The duke angrily refused to let him go and had him imprisoned for a month. The headstrong composer was eventually released in disgrace and allowed to leave Weimar with his family.

An engraving of Prince Leopold's palace at Cöthen.

THE CÖTHEN YEARS

The next few years were very happy for Bach. In August 1717, he was appointed Kapellmeister to Prince Leopold of Anhalt-Cöthen. Leopold loved music and could play the viola da gamba well. He enjoyed Bach's company and gave his family fine rooms in the palace.

Bach was hardly ever asked to write church works at Cöthen, and so he began to experiment with instrumental music. He wrote several **sonatas** and **concertos** for the violin and the flute, with flowing, song-like melodies. These show how he was influenced by the music of Italian composers. He had studied Italian music in Weimar and particularly liked the concertos of **Vivaldi**.

During this period Bach wrote six concertos dedicated to the **Margrave** of Brandenburg. The tunes are cleverly composed so that each solo instrument is shown off at its best. Prince Leopold probably played the **bass** line, while Bach liked to play the **viola**, so that he could sit right in the middle of the musicians. The *Brandenburg* Concertos are some of the greatest pieces Bach composed.

A German clavichord, 1728. Bach was especially fond of the clavichord's sweet sound.

The small group of musicians in this painting is typical of the sort that played Bach's music during the Cöthen years.

Just when everything seemed perfect, tragedy struck. Bach returned home after a trip in July 1720, to find that Maria Barbara, his wife, had died. Suddenly he was on his own after 13 years, and his four surviving children were without their mother. But 17 months later Bach married Anna Magdalena Wilcken, a 20-year-old **soprano**. Their marriage was a happy one, and Bach dedicated two special books of music to her.

Meanwhile, his two eldest boys were showing great musical talent. Bach wrote a remarkable book of keyboard pieces for them, which taught them how to play and helped them to understand music. It was called the *Well-Tempered Clavier* and was made up of 24 exercises. In music there are 24 **key signatures**, 12 **major** and 12 **minor**. In his book, Bach wrote a prelude and fugue for each one. Twenty years later he completed a second volume, again with a prelude and fugue for each key signature.

THE CLAVIER

In Bach's day the word *clavier* meant keyboard instrument, and could be used to describe both the harpsichord and the clavichord. A harpsichord's strings are plucked when the keyboard is played, which gives a bright but harsh sound. A clavichord's strings are touched by prongs from beneath, which makes a gentler sound, and Bach is said to have preferred it.

A well-tempered clavier means one that has been evenly tuned, so that the gap between each of the 12 notes in a keyboard **octave** is identical. All pianos today are well-tempered, but before Bach's time most claviers were tuned to sound perfect in only one key. The further the player traveled from that key signature, the more out of tune the music would sound. Even-tuning means that the clavier will always be very slightly out of tune, but the player is free to move from key to key. Bach's *Well-Tempered Clavier* is like a musical grammar book.

PRELUDES AND FUGUES

A prelude is a piece of music written to introduce, or go before, another work. In Bach's *Well-Tempered Clavier*, each prelude is followed by a fugue. A fugue begins with one tune played on its own. It continues, but is joined by another musical line playing exactly the same tune. Eventually there may be several lines of music, all based on the same original tune, weaving around each other at the same time.

CANTOR OF LEIPZIG

St. Thomas's School and Church, Leipzig. Bach lived and worked here for the last 27 years of his life. His family occupied rooms in the school that looked out over gardens at the edge of the town.

In December 1721, Bach's employer, Prince Leopold, got married. The new princess was not interested in music, and she began to persuade Leopold to spend less time with his musicians. Bach felt that it was time to leave Cöthen. He also wanted his older children to be near a good university. So he wrote a special cantata and used it to **audition** for the post of **cantor** at St. Thomas's Church in Leipzig. He was eager to write church music again, after 15 years in noblemen's courts, and Leipzig was his opportunity.

Leipzig was a big trading town in **Saxony**. It had no aristocratic ruler but was governed by a town council. This council offered Bach his new job in May 1723. Surprisingly, he was their third choice. They had first offered the post to the famous composer **Telemann**, but were disappointed when he turned it down.

Leipzig was one of the leading musical cities of Europe when Bach worked there. His post as cantor and music director was an important one.

As cantor, Bach had a heavy workload. He had to write and perform music each week for the town's two main churches, he had to look after the boys at St. Thomas's School, teach them music and Latin, *and* compose works for town events. He had little time to rehearse, and the musicians were mostly schoolboys. Some were let into the choir by the council even though they could not read music, which made Bach's job even more difficult.

On top of all this, there was more and more work for Bach at home as his family grew larger. Altogether he had 20 children, although only 10 lived beyond childhood. He once boasted to a friend that there was enough talent in his family to put together a choir or small orchestra.

By the age of 40, Bach was an experienced composer and one of the greatest keyboard players in Germany.

DRAMA IN CHURCH

Despite the tiring work in Leipzig, Bach still managed to be an exciting performer. He **directed** his music energetically from the violin or keyboard, and he continued to amaze people with his brilliance on the organ. As a result, he was often invited to play in neighboring towns. These trips earned him more money, but annoyed his Leipzig employers, who would have preferred an ordinary schoolmaster.

He stayed at St. Thomas's for 27 years, until the end of his life. The working conditions were difficult and Bach often thought about leaving, but there was a good side to his job as cantor. It gave him the chance to perform really large-scale works. These works used choirs, orchestra, soloists, keyboard players, and even virtuoso instrumentalists who happened to be visiting the city.

The inside of St. Thomas's Church, Leipzig, restored in 1885.

Bach put together the first of these enormous pieces for Easter 1724. It was called the *St. John Passion* and told the story of Jesus's Last Supper, trial, and Crucifixion. He wrote another in 1727 called the *St. Matthew Passion*, and both are very theatrical in style. In the music, the crowds burst out in anger, and characters such as Peter, Pilate, and Herod have their own lines to sing. A narrator tells the story, and traditional Lutheran hymns are slipped in between arias. He used the same approach in 1734 with his *Christmas Oratorio*, which tells the story of Jesus's birth.

Some people thought these works were too dramatic, and Bach was in trouble again for making church music too much like opera. But life improved for the composer when in 1730 a new rector, Johann Mattias Gesner, took over as headmaster of St. Thomas's. He respected Bach's music and managed to improve the family's uncomfortable living quarters at the school.

Bach's monogram (a kind of formal signature). He designed it himself, and it shows his initials, JSB, reading both forward and backward.

A concert at a coffeehouse. The harpsichord is right at the center of the music-making, because it provides a continuous accompaniment for the other instruments. The viola da gamba, next to the harpsichord, played the bass line, which gave a kind of musical anchor.

COFFEEHOUSE CONCERTS

Unfortunately for Bach, Gesner was replaced as Rector of St. Thomas's in 1734 by an ambitious young man called Johann August Ernesti, who thought there should be less music in the school. He constantly undermined Bach's authority and made it impossible for him to keep order with the boys. There were even scuffles in the organ loft during services. So a battle of wills broke out between the stubborn cantor and the 27-year-old rector, which lasted for years.

Bach thought of a solution. He would apply straight to the king, **Augustus III**, for a part-time appointment as court composer. He hoped that the royal title might protect him against his Leipzig employers. The plan worked. He wrote a grand Latin **mass** and dedicated the first part to the king. The Mass in B minor turned out to be one of the greatest church works ever written, and in 1736 he was at last given the royal appointment.

The problems at St. Thomas's continued, so Bach decided to spend more time composing secular music again.
In 1729 he took over as director of a group known as the **collegium musicum**, which was mostly made up of music students from the university. They met to perform on Friday evenings at a coffeehouse called Zimmermann's. Coffee was a fashionable new drink at the time, and the customers at Zimmermann's sipped from their cups, while listening to Bach and his musicians. This was something new, because in those days concerts for the ordinary people did not exist.

Bach revised some of his music from Cöthen for the collegium musicum. He wrote new works as well, including a light-hearted *Coffee Cantata*, which was probably the nearest he ever came to composing an opera.

An open-air evening concert, in summer, given by a collegium musicum.

J.A. Ernesti (1707–1781)

A NEW WAY OF THINKING

Ernesti, the new Rector of St. Thomas's, later became one of Germany's most important religious scholars. He was influenced by a new way of thinking that swept across Europe, known as the Enlightenment. In the second half of the seventeenth century, Isaac Newton discovered the law of gravity. Thinkers of the Enlightenment then began to want answers to other mysteries of the universe. They believed that they would find these answers by studying the real world and understanding it scientifically. Real freedom, they claimed, would come through education and learning, not religious superstitions.

For some people, such as Ernesti, church music was not part of a sensible, thinking approach to God, because it played too much on people's feelings. The Enlightenment encouraged people to think for themselves. Eventually it also led them to realize that they had rights and could rebel against **oppressive** rulers.

THE OLD MASTER

A portrait of Carl Philipp Emanuel Bach, who spent most of his life working at the court of Frederick the Great.

Bach was one of the greatest music teachers of all time. He wrote many student pieces, particularly for the keyboard. In one of his last compositions, *The Art of Fugue*, he explores the most complicated ways of using fugues and canons. It is the work of an old master, passing on his learning to future generations.

Five of his sons were outstanding musicians. One of them, Carl Philipp Emanuel (1714–1788), was court musician to Frederick the Great, the young King of Prussia. He arranged for his father to visit the royal court in Potsdam. When Bach arrived, Frederick, who had been playing the flute, stopped and announced, "Gentlemen, Old Bach is here!"

The composer played for him and later wrote a special *Musical Offering* based on a tune written by the king himself. He included a sonata for flute and violin in this work for Frederick to play.

By 1750 Bach had begun to work less, partly because he was not so interested in his duties as cantor and partly because his eyesight was failing. In the end he agreed to have two operations on his eyes rather than go blind. There were no **anesthetics** in those days, and the pain must have been unbearable. The operations were a failure and Bach's health quickly became much worse. He was ill for three months and died on July 28, 1750.

A concert at Frederick the Great's palace, Potsdam. The King is shown playing the flute.

FREDERICK THE GREAT (1712–1786)

Frederick the Great of Prussia was a good musician and was interested in writing and philosophy. He became a friend of leading Enlightenment figures, such as the French writer **Voltaire**. Bach's son, C.P.E. Bach, was his court musician for nearly 30 years.

Frederick was also the most successful general of his time and a political reformer. When he became king in 1740, he allowed more freedom and made torture illegal. But he introduced high taxes to pay for a series of wars against Austria. During one of these wars, in 1745, his troops occupied Leipzig, the town where Bach lived, for a short time.

By the end of his reign, Prussia was twice as big as it had been and had a mighty army of 200,000 men. Frederick had broken Austria's control over northern Europe, and because of this the single country we now call Germany was eventually created.

BACH LIVES ON

As a boy, Wilhelm Friedemann Bach (above) was his father's pride and joy. Although very talented, he did not have his father's strong sense of discipline. In later life, he even tried to pretend that some of his father's less well-known works were his own. His life was full of disappointment, and little remains of his own music.

ach was buried in St. John's Cemetery, Leipzig. His body was dug up in 1894, when scientists confirmed that it was the composer's, and then again in 1950, when it was moved to St. Thomas's Church.

Anna Magdalena was treated rather badly by her stepchildren and was left with little money. She died in poverty ten years after her husband.

Apart from Carl Philipp Emanuel, three of Bach's other sons became famous musicians. The eldest, Wilhelm Friedemann (1710–1784), was a good composer and brilliant organist, but he never settled into a secure job, and died penniless. Johann Christoph Friedrich (1732–1795) became a court musician in Bückeburg, and Johann Christian (1735–1782) was a very successful composer, who lived in England. They all realized that their father was a great man, but their own music belonged to a new style. Bach's music began to sound out of date.

Johann Christian Bach became one of the best-loved composers of his day. For a time he was organist at Milan Cathedral in Italy. He then moved to London where he became music teacher to the royal family. He was a great favorite in England and remained there until his death. He also met and influenced the great composer Mozart, who visited London as a child.

The 1960s band, the Beatles, borrowed ideas from classical music for their songs.

Some composers, such as Mozart, Haydn, and Beethoven, appreciated Bach, but he did not become really well known again for many years. In 1829 the composer **Felix Mendelssohn**, aged only 20, conducted a performance of the *St. Matthew Passion*—the first since Bach's death.

After that, Bach's surviving works were published, and they have been performed all over the world ever since.
The influence of his style can be heard in some pop music, such as the trumpet tune in "Penny Lane" by the Beatles and the piano solo in Nina Simone's "My Baby Just Cares for Me."

A special tribute to Bach's greatness is thousands of miles away in space. In 1977 the *Voyager* spacecraft was launched with a gold-plated record on board, ready to play if the craft should ever meet life on another planet. The first communication representing humans to extraterrestrials is Bach's *Brandenburg* Concerto no. 2.

The *Voyager* spacecraft setting off on its long journey into the unknown in 1977, with music by Bach on board.

TIME CHART

1685 Johann Sebastian Bach born in Eisenach, March 21.

1694 Bach's mother, Elisabeth, dies. Buried May 3.

1695 Bach's father, Johann Ambrosius dies, February 20. Bach moves to his brother's cottage in Ohrdruf.

1700 Bach attends St. Michael's School, Lüneburg, until 1702.

1701 War of the Spanish Succession begins (and continues until 1714).

1703 Bach appointed organist at New Church in Arnstadt, August 9.

1707 Bach appointed organist at the Church of St. Blaise, Mühlhausen, June 15. Marriage to Maria Barbara Bach, October 17.

1708 Bach appointed organist and chamber musician to the court of Duke Wilhelm Ernst of Saxe-Weimar.

1710 Birth of son, Wilhelm Friedemann, November 22.

1712 Birth of Frederick the Great.

1714 Birth of son, Carl Philipp Emanuel, March 8.

1717 Bach imprisoned, and eventually released to take up appointment as Kapellmeister at the court of Prince Leopold of Anhalt-Cöthen.

1720 Maria Barbara dies. Buried July 7.

1721 Bach marries Anna Magdalena Wilcken, December 3.

1723 Bach appointed cantor at St. Thomas's Church, Leipzig, May 5.

1729 Bach takes over directorship of collegium musicum.

1732 Birth of son, Johann Christoph Friedrich, June 21.

1733 Bach applies for appointment as royal court composer.

1735 Birth of son, Johann Christian, September 5.

1736 Bach finally appointed royal court composer.

1740 Frederick the Great becomes King of Prussia, and goes to war with Austria (until 1748).

1745 Leipzig invaded by Prussian troops.

1747 Bach visits Frederick the Great's court at Potsdam.

1750 Bach undergoes eye surgery (March–April), and dies, July 28. Buried, July 30, in St. John's Cemetery, Leipzig.

GLOSSARY

anesthetic A special drug used by doctors to lower the level of pain felt by people during operations.

aria A song for a solo singer. Aria is the Italian for "air," which is also a musical term for "tune."

audition A test given to performing musicians to see how good they are.

Augustus III (1696–1763) Augustus was the Elector, or ruler, of Saxony. In 1733, with the help of the Holy Roman Emperor, he was chosen to be the new King of Poland, and Saxony was included as part of his kingdom. He is remembered as a supporter of the arts.

bass The lowest note, line, or instrument in a musical grouping. The bass note forms the anchor, or foundation, for musical harmony.

Bernini, Gian Lorenzo (1598–1680) Italian sculptor and architect of the Baroque. He built large parts of the Vatican in Rome, and became the most important sculptor of his day, concentrating on portraits and religious works.

Buxtehude, Dietrich (1637–1707) Composer and organist who developed the style of organ music that Bach imitated and perfected.

cantor The director of music at a German Protestant church.

ceremonial An event that is grand, public, or sacred, and that is usually marked by special traditions (or ceremonies).

choral scholarship A place at a school offered to someone who sings very well. In return for free education the choral scholar sings in the school's choir.

chorale Hymn, or hymn tune, used by Lutherans as an important part of church worship.

chorister A person who sings in a choir.

collegium musicum A group of professional and student musicians who met regularly in eighteenth-century German towns to perform secular music.

concerto A piece of music written for orchestra and solo instruments.

counterpoint A musical line written or played alongside another of equal importance. (See polyphony.)

direct In Bach's day music would be directed, rather than conducted, by a performer, usually on the violin or at the keyboard. He would lead the other musicians with his own playing and the occasional gesture.

duchy The area ruled by a duke.

fugue A fugue is a piece of music that begins with a tune played on its own. It develops, but is joined by another musical line playing the same tune as at the start, and so on. There can be several lines, all based on the original tune, weaving around one another.

guild A group of people who all do the same job and help one another in difficult times.

improvise To compose music while performing it, rather than playing from memory or from written music.

Kapellmeister The senior musician at the court of a ruler or aristocrat.

key signature A way of grouping written music into different "families." Each key signature is known by a letter (A, B, C, D, E, F, and G), together with variations ("sharp" and "flat," "major" and "minor"). There are 24 key signatures altogether, and the music sounds higher or lower, depending on which one is used.

Luther, Martin (1483–1546) Scholar and leader of the religious Reformation, who broke ties with the Pope in 1517 and founded a new Church in Germany—the Lutheran Church. His followers are Protestants.

Magnificat The Latin words to the song sung by the Virgin Mary, which begins "My soul doth magnify the Lord."

major and **minor** Two different ways of treating the same key signature. In general, a minor key, because of the notes it uses, has a sad or solemn feel, whereas a major key sounds bright and positive.

margrave A title for a certain kind of German aristocrat.

mass An important part of church worship in the Christian religion. Many composers have set the mass to music.

melody A tune.

Mendelssohn, Felix (1809–1847) German composer. He showed outstanding talent at a very young age and had composed a number of masterpieces by the age of 16. He became very popular in Britain.

octave The eight notes of a musical scale. All key signatures, major and minor, are based on an octave scale, starting with one note (for example, C), going through the next six (D, E, F, G, A, B), and moving on to C again. The final C is the same note as the first, but is an octave higher.

opera A musical drama in which the performers sing most or all of their lines, usually accompanied by an orchestra.

oppressive A way of ruling that uses cruelty and injustice to control people.

oratorio A large-scale musical work involving solo singers, orchestra, and chorus. Oratorios are usually based on religious subjects.

Pietist A person who belonged to a strict religious movement that began in Lutheran Germany in the seventeenth century. Pietists believed that a person's life and work should be completely dedicated to God, and that the Bible was the only true guide.

polyphony Music that has several musical lines, of equal importance, weaving around one another at the same time, rather than one main tune line. (See counterpoint.)

prelude A piece of music written to introduce, or go before, another piece.

Protestant The name given to people (or Churches) who have separated themselves from the power of the Pope and the Roman Catholic Church.

Prussia A powerful state in northeast Germany ruled by the Hohenzollern family. When Germany eventually became a single country, the Prussian royal family ruled as emperors.

recitative A piece of speech set to music, in which the words are more important than the tune. A recitative usually introduces an aria.

Reich The collection of German states that made up the empire.

Saxony A state in central Germany.

secular Nonreligious, or belonging to the world outside the Church.

sonata A piece of music written for the keyboard or for another solo instrument accompanied by the keyboard.

soprano The highest voice of the five main types of singers (the others are alto, tenor, baritone, and bass).

Telemann, Georg Philipp (1681–1767) In his day, Telemann was considered the most distinguished composer, Kapellmeister, and director of church music in Germany.

Thirty Years' War (1618–1648) This began as a war between Catholic and Protestant royalty in northern Europe, but developed into a power struggle between France and the Hapsburg family, which ruled Germany and Spain. The war ended with the Treaty of Westphalia.

toccata A form of music that takes its name from the Italian *toccare*, "to touch." It is used to describe a type of keyboard music that requires a quick touch of the finger.

variations Different musical versions of an original tune.

viola A string instrument placed under the chin and played with a bow. A viola is larger than a violin, and the sound it produces is deeper. It comes between the violin and the viola da gamba (or cello).

viola da gamba An early string instrument placed between the knees and played with a bow. It produced a deep sound (see bass). In recent times it has been replaced by the cello.

virtuoso A particularly skillful performer on his or her chosen instrument.

Vivaldi, Antonio (1678–1741) Italian composer who lived in Venice. He wrote a vast number of concertos and was a distinguished violinist.

Voltaire, François (1694–1778) A leading French author of the Enlightenment. He was known for his humor and his lifelong fight against the injustice of oppressive rulers.

INDEX